WORDPLANTING

ACKNOWLEDGEMENTS

Many thanks to the following in which a few of these poems appeared:

BIM: "A Birthday Reflection in Verse for Fidel", "Tea".

Clean Slate: "Herons".

So Many Islands: "Avocado".

Griffith Review 59: "Avocado".

KENDEL HIPPOLYTE

WORDPLANTING

P E E P A L   T R E E

First published in Great Britain in 2019
Peepal Tree Press Ltd
17 King's Avenue
Leeds LS6 1QS
UK

ISBN 13: 9781845234355

Supported using public funding by
ARTS COUNCIL
ENGLAND

CONTENTS

A LETTER FOR SOLIDARITY

Dear Marie,

The slogans have garbled down to gibbering ads,
the rallying songs crackled flat into statistics;
the visionary icons and ideograms have shrunk
into abbreviations: P&L, GDP;
our dazed, mall-eyed children feed on cyberflakes
whizzed up in a billion glass-and-plastic boxes;
and we all work now in the fastest growing industry,
the invisible service sector of our spiritual death.
Marie, how did we come to work so diligently at our dying?
To try so doggedly to buy a meaningful existence
on an instalment plan, arrange for happiness on hire purchase?
What thinned and fizzed and saccharined our blood
that in the grip and shake of life we gushed bubbling inanities?
And what are we now? Cassettes already on the B-side,
songs slurring down back into obsolete machines
playing in small rooms these selfsame last sounds cannot fill.
i would weep for both of us, for our generation,
if tears could flow inward, sting the bloodflow to the flabbed heart,
flood the scabbed roads of compromise we made to end up here.
But what tears can dissolve asphalt on the inner roads
scraped through and sneered across the heart's land?
What regret now can rewrite, truthfully, the words
shouting on placards that we eventually dropped somewhere?
All we can hope for now is understanding, more enduring, solid,
than the cardboard signs softening in rain, bleaching in sun,
that peeled, then sloughed their markings off. The last failure.

Or the first. For isn't the understanding why we failed
the understanding we should have begun with
to have saved us from failure? More, wasn't its shape
with us then, in our foreshadows on the asphalt?
We trailed their vanguard flittering to the rallies, barricades,

our heads high, looking up to progress; we did not look down
to common ground where we all cast the same shape
as a policeman with no baton, a soldier with no gun.
That shape, which flowed with an innate decorum, i remember,
from a deeply considerate, deeply conservative, fellow student
whom i reluctantly respected even then (you noticed),
as he and i walked, arguing, late afternoon light at our backs,
the loomings of our shadows leaking from us,
going ahead of our feet, the same ungraspable
dark forms no one could colour or pin a badge on.

Marie, what if – on the left side of the barricaded gates then,
looking each other into selfsame solidarity,
looking them, the other side, into a uniformed enmity –
what if we'd lowered our fierce regard to ground?
What would the stark glyphs there have shown?
Morning, midday, late afternoon, our dark imagos lengthening
beyond the metal, wire-meshed gates, attenuating
toward them, then theirs toward us.

Decades, and the same uncertaining shadows, years longer,
are moving charcoal sketches of a subject we still do not know.
The long obscurities of self always silhouette ahead of us –
in silence, before the words we hold loudly over our heads.
Unacknowledged, they reach our destinations, touch them
before we do, shade them into destiny. We do not think it so,
but in our unacknowledgement, the shadows act, our actions follow.
But to know this, act in knowledge of it, is the understanding
more elusive than a shadow that we needed then
and – so that our children do not become our shadows –
that we need   more   always   ever   now.

In hope of solidarity, Marie

K.

HARP

(for Loretta Collins-Klobah)

Where the rivers of Babylon clog into vomit,
curdling in the high, blind-white, concrete gully
behind the salvage-wood and galvanize-sheet tenement,
i hang my harp upon a half-burnt post lean-out over a zinc-fence corner
and leave it there – to dry-rot, crack, split,
for the strings to snap, flail, hang down
like a locksman beard below a face empty of everything,
so as to hurt a warning, a reminder, deep into my spirit.

Because even my own people did say unto me: "Oy! Stop it!
Nuh budda bring no lamentations round bout ya.
You ever hear a harp play dancehall? Even reggae?
Is how you a-go strum militant 'pon something so
wha' play so sweet? So sad? Yo! Elder! Res' it up."

And in truth, they set my spirit wondering:
because, yes, at Jericho, was rams' horns blasting,
reggae guitar chopping, one drop-one chop, at the foundation,
bass bucking like a battering ram 'gainst gates of oppression
and Gideon boots trodding the rhythm seven times round
did make the weak-heart walls to tremble and crash down.
No harp that time did make one single sound. Is true.

But after the walls bow down to us, after the city fall, is wha' we do?
Take the same stones, Babylon fool's-gold brick,
and build, more hard heart than concrete, wall after wall
within the midst of us, dividedness upon dividedness.
Our stiff-neck high ways snub out paths that we did walk
and every cross road where your spirit turn, a block.
Warriors untie their Gideon boots to walk on carpet, ride sleek chariot.
Princes' daughters drape their selves in Babylon ol' bruk.
We smile and manacle each other's hands and feet in shekels
and cash-and-carry us into captivity, chinking in coffles our selves did make,
shuffling between walls of gold that we refuse to climb – or break.

Is why our children, though they doan know,
gnash at each other; why their songs sometimes does snarl
like male dog fighting; or whimper like a bitch in heat;
why the guitar is a self-reloading rifle screaming *Shatta!*;
bass is a 12-guage bucky random in the dancehall;
and drum and cymbal in a 'tomp and slash, both getting beat.
They trying to batter their way through. But that kinda wall
that we make our self, it doan fall so. It have to melt.
Something have to slip through. From below.
Was why I start play harp. Let water ripple
from a new musical uprising, undermind, let truth flow,
loose the foundation, sunder the blocks of gold, stone after stone,
until the whole unholy God-forsaking kingdom fall.

So i start play, plucking the tight strings at my breast,
sitting under a hillside tree outside the glinting walls.
Then potholes in the city streets blink into eyes filling with water
and water tremoloing at each note, beginning to brim over, spill,
sipple below the cars, uprise from the gutters, seek into buildings, searching.
And i, wet-eyed elder, see what used to be man, woman, even children,
coffling out, stark-staring into clear truth rising around them,
staring back at shadows in the water, ghost and phantom
wavering upward and wailing without sound for their lost substance.
And my fingers grappling the harp's heart-strings, trengling, hurting,
but I yearning the water up to overflow, the cup of raging sorrow to run over,
to break banks, break Babel Tower, break Babylon crooked edifices,
break the i-dazzling barriers, the cold-gold-gleaming walls between us
down. I pray my harp unceasing, clutch at the cords, the lifelines of that music,
my fingers failing and unfailing, note after note, year after year.

And after a time, and then a time again, I hear
voices. Each one bringing it own sound, it singling vibration:
one, like a boulder unburdening from a hillside, dragging gravel down,
rockstone rackling a way through, restless, rolling, brash – till Shiloh;
one, like the fine substance of archangels' bodies, something in it higher
than the ear, and if eye could see it, woulda sheer, strong, clear – like silk;

one, like an announcing from around a hill, a shout of light, and then
sun striking bright notes glittering off a staff – of an approaching messenger.
I was hearing other voices too, like small streams and rills
just after a big rain. A righteousness was trickling through,
bubbling from the sound systems, flowing out of little studios into the streets, the gullies,
even up to the gated cemeteries of the half-dead on the hills of Babylon.
Voices. Answering-I-calling, allowing I to lay the burden,
to refrain, cease my sole harping, let i and **i** and **I**, all,
carrying each part true, whole the new song.

Doh seem so long ago, all that. And is not dream I dream it.
For the I doh dream. I vision.
So where all that go?
i shake my head all now – the question still rattling in it.
No answer. But I know
the day the water, with no warning, cease it cleansing flow;
my eyes prickle, I hear fire roaring, hear a high, rending scream
like something rip, then tearing slow. Then word spread
to every tenement, to each heart-door, how he run back
into the hot howling of his burning home, run back,
his own voice beginning to singe, run back
toward his mother in the wailing smoke and flame
and Garnett dead.

So same harp i did lay down, i take up again.
Street corner, market place, every quick footpath between yard and yard,
i there calling again the water – river and drain, each bucketful and cup we have,
to pour on our scorched ground, quench out the conflagration raging again within
even the little ones, red-eye already from the consuming inflammation
that the archangel music was a cool balm and healing for.
i play, i lion-paw and claw the strings, i scrabbling to catch the water
falling in trickles in the harp. But now, more and more, my fingers clenching
at a slow silence that they cannot hold, drying closer, even unto the I.

Was in that time the young men and women, even children,
started to cast the pebbles of their words: "Yo, elder! Stop it!

Nuh budda bring no Lamentations round 'bout ya."
Pebbles, true, not rockstone, not so heavy-hearting. Still
their words fall clattering on the rooftop of my meditation,
rattling my spirit. Because if they don't want the water of this music,
how will they slake the thirst, the fevering after things, the flames of always wanting?
That's what I try to play to them, my splayed fingers beckoning come, come,
my head leaning out to listen, my spirit stretching out to catch and hold –
however, whenever it will come – the strain, again, of the new song.
Then sudden so, rockstone and boulder fall and crash onto my roof,
though is only this man coulda hear them, only this man I-sight see
the salt-white little stones rattling downward into heaps, then the heaps crumbling
into slick lines of dead white crystal dust. Word roll through later:
the singer with the voice of grit and gravel, who had been journeying to Shiloh,
take a wrong turn, follow a track into the Sheol-house they set up for him,
his voice now whispering down to silence for want of this same water.

And in my harp now, only thin tricklings, a slow dripping. Slower.
i was wizening into the dry-eyed elder, squinting into the wind for signs,
wanting but fearing what the I may see, listening and wanting not to,
hoping for news, hoping for no news. Pondering the messenger.
i pick a string … the next … nick at another … nail-scrape the one after … scratch
to pluck the air hiding in the spaces in between … i flick … wait for the flow …
The loudest sound. Is no sound. It can deaf you. But harder still
is, after that, to stroke, one last time, one last luck, the littlest string – and hear,
trembling back, the song you thought that had refrained from you the last time.
Because after that, sun-evening to moon-morning, i roaming the tenement,
at each hard door plucking each heart-door handle, looking within, listening,
though no sound calling back to me but tenement voices: "Oy! Stop it!
People just want sleep! Go back to your gates, old man!"
Is not one time or two they say it. But woulda never matter, still,
how often. I listening, past their words, for the sound of water, rippling.
Now i holding the harp tighter, thirsting, pulling the thin, slack strings
of my own spittle. My spirit stretch, lean far, far in … The twang of dry.
And in the yard, the heat of always hungering, for bread, for baubles,
was smouldering in all eyes, shrivelling empty hands to brittle tinder twigs:
"Yo, elder! End it now. Dem times done. Look to your gates, old man."

Is not one time or two they say it. "Look to your gates …"
Even to this day, my mind still embering. And is not so much
the red crackling of how, the grey wisps of who, the hot, breaking hurt of why,
but: Is how come I-lumination, who always before did light up, over head, my way
left me to walk the crooked mile back from the unseeing Saturday market glare
to the red gash flaring at the zinc-fence corner where my house was shrinking,
trying to hide from the consuming blaze – devouring hearts, far less a house.
Siren was wailing closer and a line of neighbours shuffling bucketfuls of water
but i flail past them. For I know. To quench the fire within that start this fire,
it take a different flow. So – smell of dreadlocks burning, the screaming of skin blistering,
i ravage my way in, i salvage from the flames my harp, dripping the last hopefuls of water.

They tell me i was lying in the wet ash and black, smoking shards
under my roof that crash and cover me, holding so tight the harp,
they woulda have to break my fingers. So they left us there.
Sun-fire burn out, moon rain her light down, my spirit cool, my harp dry quiet.
And morning come, sun flickering, the other heat starting again, a red rash
itching through ghetto, guard-gate entrances, high-up windows – the consuming heat.
i get up, only half-listening for the messenger; i walk between the tenement voices,
look to my gates. The empty there was larger than the whole yard.
i hang my harp upon a half-burnt post lean-out over a zinc-fence corner
and leave it there.

A BIRTHDAY REFLECTION IN VERSE FOR FIDEL

From the Sierra Maestra heights of your eighty-five years
what do you see when you look back
at the long journey, always uphill, that has brought you here?
This journey that began as a young man's fierce, questing track
through the unending campesino poverty and Habana's corrupt streets and palaces where
Uncle Sam's Mafia nephews gambled for Cuba with goons and profiteers.

What do you see, El Commandante, when you scrutinise
a more than half-century of revolucion?
Green fields of schoolchildren; muralled workplaces; the shared grain of material progress;
a peasant unbending upward, exclamation mark from his own question;
and between Moncada and Playa Giron, a people finding a lost consciousness.
Such memories no doubt must fill and overbrim your eyes.

But you see too the shadows of the clouds over your island:
thunderheads swelling; a threatening nuclear rain;
a fifty-two year siege; a bomb-barrage of lies; a strangling embargo;
638 assassination plots (and even now they still would try again);
a static swarm of truth-obscuring flies; the continuing insult of Guantanamo.
Yet Cuba's history remains; imperial waves of onslaught ebb into sand.

You faced the same devil-and-deep sea dilemmas Toussaint came upon,
determining who the ally, who the enemy.
Like him, you struggled, almost lost, then broke the rack
your country suffered on, undid the golden shackles. Then when she was free,
met the irrational rage of the defeated master who wants his slave-mistress back.
It's what they all want, whether the star-spangled emperors or Napoleon.

All this must be so clear from your Sierra Maestra height
i wonder how Cuba now seems from that view:
a young woman at a mirror, beautiful, trembling with unmade decisions;
a daughter, half-wanting to leave home and aching with her fidelity to you.
In a car outside, Uncle and Madam wait, with gold anklets and white, powdery persuasions.
Cuba, in a fierce trembling at the mirror, eyes searching left, then right.

i'm trembling too. Till i remind myself: you raised her. Very well.
She'll know how to keep both eyes open,
to walk a path without the signposts you had, but still with your vision.
She'll show a way for her scattered archipelago family who have kept hope in
her, in Caribbean civilization. Her history, El Jefe, has been your absolution.
Cuba, señor, is your best gift to yourself. And us. A happy 85th, Fidel.

AVOCADO
(for Gordon Rohlehr)

i woke one morning and the Caribbean was gone.
She'd definitely been there the night before, i'd heard her
singing in crickets and grasshoppers to the tambourine of the oncoming rain.
A childhood song. i slept down into childhood.
i woke blinking in a null glare without sunbeams, with no winkling motes,
all things bright and 20/20 visible in neon but unilluminated.
And though the finches, doves, banana quits, tremblers, grackles, mocking birds
sang to each other still, the music ended when their singing ended.
Not like the day before when what they sang were motifs in an overture,
a maypole reeling and unreeling of ourselves and other selves of nature
swirling out into a futuriginal symphony of civilization entitling itself Caribbean.

i thought: she can't be gone. If she is gone,
what is this place? With her gone, who am i?
If she is gone, who braids the fraying fibres of memory into accord?
Traces the beach footprints of our children back to the first tracks of the Ciboney?
Who plaits the scattered flowers of islands and sprigs of continent into a votive wreath
cast in appeasement on the ocean restless with the unrestituted dead,
to sea us into the altering calm of Sunday mornings, trees in surplices of light
and the allaying litany of the waves' asking and the sand's assenting?
i thought: She isn't gone, just hidden. i'll go find her.
And so i went looking.

i went first to the beach, of course, remembering
how she loved fluidities, the wavering margins of the sand and water,
the way that wind could soothe the stinging of the sun's ray's –
the original elements, she'd said, dwelling within themselves while intermingling.
But at the beach, the barricades of deck chairs, ramparts of pastel walls
blocked any wandering. A non-pastel guard, though, told me he'd glimpsed her
walking off between clipped hedges that closed after her into a maze,
tatters of madras hanging where there used to be hibiscus.
There had been rumours of hotel managers trying to hire the sunlight,
contract the hurricane into a breeze for gently fluttering brochures,

draw columns of strict profit margins permanently on the sand;
and the Caribbean, sensing the intimation of quick, crab-like hands crawling
to get underneath the white broderie anglaise of her skirt, withdrew herself
the way the sea, clenching herself into a tidal wave, withdraws.

i left the beach, wondering my way back toward a town still struggling toward a city,
looking for her, as i used to, in an unexpectedness of roadside flowers,
a sudden glorying of croton plashing against a low grey house,
a slump of cane leaning into the road, just so, beside a shack.
And it was strange, their way now of receding from me while remaining.

Into the town, following the fadeout track of a child's footsteps into memory
or perhaps trailing the under-scent of hot molasses, her history's black sweat,
i dipped into the volatile conviviality of rumshops, their ricochet of dominoes,
cracking reports of man-to-man talk, the slam of coins on counter,
brawling laughter half an inch short of a fight, the bottle tipping, rum-settling everything –
the rituals exactly as they were when i was nine and she'd walked the whole neighbourhood.
I asked the rum acolytes, who unbowed their heads from drinks and dominoes and swore
she'd just been there, just! They asked me where she'd gone!

i left them in a spluttering fusillade of words about who'd seen her last,
and stepped into a Saturday morning of a market hopscotched with vendors,
their come-to-me calls crisscrossing in a birdflight chattering,
their seasonings, vegetables, fruits set out in clusters – breves, crochets, minims
of aubergine, pomerac, thyme along the staves of foodpaths – and i thought:
Surely, somewhere within this kente-tartan-madras self-arranging medley,
this market women melody within sound and smell of the hot pepper sizzling of Accra,
i will find her? And, tell you the truth, there was one moment.

A woman, sitting thighs akimbo, the cascade of her wide blue skirt
falling towards the plenitude she'd gathered from her hillside garden,
from the abundance of her country where land is still the earth,
called out to me, one hand holding the green orb of an avocado:
"Solinah friend! For you."
And then the ceremonies of thanks, gracious inquiries, regards, "Ba-bye."
And somewhere in this intermingling, though i didn't know the moment:

between her fingers loosening and mine tightening around
(both of us holding, neither of us quite owning)
what she was giving me, what i was accepting, in that green present
which i received really only later that day when i'd stopped looking,
and realization ripened like a fruit or vegetable or whatever people call an avocado.

i left the market and the moment without knowing
where my feet were going or should go or if there was a where
that i could go to in the certainty of finding her.
i walked, all i could do was walk.
The streets still knew each other's names, met at corners, exchanged views –
St Louis gossiping with Coral, Marchand Road turning to Riverside,
joined in one conversation till Mary Ann, then Brazil, interrupted –
but fewer people heard them – their chat, their names, dispersed to whispers
in the snarl of vehicles revving further north to Rodney Heights, to Cap Estate,
to NY 00001…

i stood at a crossroads, squinting at the oncoming rush of cars wearing
wraparound dark glasses,
trying to see into them in case someone had taken her for a ride.
i failed. Too fast, too loud, too tinted. Not just cars. The whole thing.
i kept walking.
I passed the downtown, quick-change, wannabe boutiques with glitzy accessories,
the young women inside clickety-jangling glass beads, ankle chains, slave bangles,
themselves accessories of the unravelling tawdry evening dress of empire;
past the cave mouths of the games arcades, their gnash and screeling in a dimness
juddering with the silhouettes of our children transmogrified into Ameritrons.
i recognised my son's friend; his eyes clicked; de-recognised me; i kept walking.

The slow lemon light of the hours after work, accumulated week-long,
slid down the sides of buildings drained of meaning on a Saturday afternoon;
incipient growth of evening shadow on the facades of stores, banks, offices;
the crick of faces loosening their rictuses; the after-sound of slackening footsteps
going home. And something still undone, unfelt. Missed. Where was she?
And if in truth she had gone – the centuries of her civilising presence, in the air like sea salt,
the cascade of good years like grains of rice pouring from cup to pot, generations
of her mothering, neighbouring, villaging, lend-hand, raising up, lifting up

our eyes higher than empty hands closing into tight fists to scratch an itch of silver –
if after all this, she had gone, what wider absence was there left to know
except the sky-wide absence of our not even knowing?

So now – walk home? Sun winking red, last minutes of battery life … Walk home.
Same house. Yet not. It too has receded into the elsewhere of the intimate distance
with the crotons, the cane stalks near the shack, the greying flower-flecked road,
into the infinitesimal distance between longing memory and a wanting present.
Open the door. Walk into displacement. Sit at a kitchen table. Stare
at a half-curled hand of bananas, some knuckles of turmeric, straw basket
clutching tomatoes…
The wisp of a remembered argument – Is tomato a vegetable or fruit? –
reminds you of the avocado in your backpack. The gift from her, a woman
whom you didn't know and who did not know you but you both knew Solinah.

And somewhere along the arc out of my bag onto the kitchen table, the avocado
ripened into me: in the hot haggling of the market, a gift between two strangers
for her sake. In the green globe of one moment, the seed of a whole civilization.

Really? Had a market woman, hand raised with a gift, from her to me through
Solinah, in that casual gesture traced the curving line that rounds into community?
Romanticism, surely? Yet how else, through centuries of the stock exchange of flesh
– glistened black bodies ⇌ tarnished silver coins transacted on an auction block –
how else had the bought-and-sold survived within their own unchatteled selves?
Gift. The unslaved remembering of hands held out with no calculating fingers, offering
the graciousness that grows out of a ground of knowing: existence is a grace.
Grace eliding into graciousness eliding into gift. The first fruits of civilization.

And since that glimpse, like a green flash, i've seen her, the Caribbean,
in unexpected places. Her visitations are a gleam and then a dimming:
a far hillside district, descendant of a freetown settlement, in the mid-day light;
or a glint of zinc from a house changing half of its roof on a Saturday half-day, given
to a koudmen, lend-hand, gayap, koumbit, fajina, jollification, maroon, gotong rojong,
or whatever people say to try to nail with names the element beyond grasp, above our heads,
holding the sheltering restored roof of community in place. Harder to find now,
and when found, best held lightly, in an open palm; then unheld, let go
in an unexpected, unexpecting, freehand green thankful of avocado.

DOMESTICITIES – 1: TEA

As a child, watching my mother cool the hot tea by pouring it
from one cup into another, then from the filled cup back
into the emptied one, and then again, again,
the afternoon-or-evening-coloured liquid unfurling downward
like a ribbon from a spool, the sound of its unreeling
an ascending-then-descending octave ending in a burbling,
then a clustering of bubbles, and the vapour wisping
from and to my mother's hands gliding up, down, changing places,
partners in an intricate and courtly dance, separating finally
when she passed me the cup, the porcelain at just the hotness
to allow my other hand to support it at the rim as i raise to my lips
the tea – kannèl, Red Rose, lowanjèt – hotter than the cup, just
to the right sweetened heat for a child learning to sip, absorb
the ways of family, of neighbourhood, of town, of country – a child
wondering two generations later when precisely this ritual
became unnecessary, wondering how i learned to drink tea hot
and wondering whether the hands of any of us still dance
the caring choreography of this domestic rite,
wondering if they do not, why …

DOMESTICITIES – 2: HOUSE MUSIC

Snare brush of a broom sets up a rhythm,
kettledrum clatter of the plates and cups in counterpoint,
cymbal clash of dishwater sloshed out through a kitchen doorway,
finger-snapping hectic clacking of the house wares
washed-rinsed-racked-dripping-dry –
song done started.
Bright golden sizzling opening notes scatting around inside a skillet,
cup filling from a tap trills rapidly up and down a silver octave –
even the wrong note squeaking of a door fits right in, just swinging
right there with the tinkling of spoons, the saucepans clanking,
bebop bass voice of peas bubbling in a big pot.
Man, this song is cooking!
The real house music,
music of home

DOMESTICITIES – 3: *POET*

He carries his home with him – always, like a snail its shell.
He is attached to it. It fastens to his very body.
In the mind's terrain of uncertainty, on a rough stone path of words
along which he must make his journeying to he knows not where,
the shell is shelter, retreat, a shape he pulls his self into.
Inside the familial contours of the house whorled round him,
he rests – until a twitch of the unknown, a fleck of perhaps rain,
stirs him back toward the doorway, where he pauses – stalks one hand out,
another, leaning half-out, looking; alert as the antennae of a snail
listening for the quivering air, the call stronger than the impulse that pulls back
the questing flesh into the self-enclosing spiral, the safe, securing clasp of home.
Shivering, he steps out, unsettling the shape that he was, half under the lintel,
and walks out of familiarity into the uncertainty he needs as he resumes his journeying –
as a snail does, carrying his home with him.

DOMESTICITIES – 4: *THE FITNESS OF THINGS*

The symmetries of household:
how chairs fit into the spaces under tables, waiting;
a glass of cold water placed, lifted, placed back
into the wet translucent circle it has made;
a shirt on a hanger, holding its shape
till you unhang it, slip it onto you,
clasp it with buttons, fill it;
the opened window, framing branches and leaves
into a painting only now discovered;
the nooks behind doors as they open;
floors waiting for a footfall;
the whole house, even when empty,
occupied by its expectancies;
holding itself together, awaiting inhabitance.

You, making the bed,
the fluffed falling of the fading-blue sheet, at its lower end,
as i walk through the bedroom doorway
and you are about to bend and tuck a corner under.
What is it
that moves my hands to reach for, pull the opposite corner
tight, unrumple the other end of the sheet upward
without thinking, soothe its wrinklings to a soft flatness?
What is it
— effortless, easily missed —
matching my movements to yours across the mattress
we make into a bed?

DOMESTICITIES – 6: *FO' DAY MORNING*
(for Jane)

In the fo' day morning dark, you scoop and tip three teaspoonfuls
into the coffee pot, you slow-walk to the stove, you strike a match
and the incandescent blue chrysanthemum of the lit gas ring
blooms instantly. And then you wait
until the low grumble of the liquid burbling, the smell of coffee coming toward you
across the room, now stirring with the sunlight sifting through the jalousies.
You pour, into a small brown cup older than you are but unchanged,
a fluent, black and gold-gleamed flow, offering its heat, the bitter truth-taste of itself.
Your lips, the mouth of this cup meet, you sip deep into you
not only the morning coffee but the morning:
the cool floor, withholding its gleam till you have opened a door or window,
the snuffling of the two small dogs shifting again into a yet more comfortable slump,
the easy distance back into the room in which you'd softly left
your wife curved in a zigzag under the covers in half-sleep:
all brewed in the percolator, all wafting up at you now as you lift the cup.

Later, in the harrying of a purposeful, brisk lunch hour,
this can be blinked away. But from the true perspective
of the half-dark, held-in light of fo' day morning, you can see
the simple elements of your life emerge from dimness, settle around you,
settle into you, settle you, so that slowly you feel your life
coming to home.

AT MOUNT SINAI MEDICAL CENTER, FLORIDA
(for Jane)

Miami: buildings and people fresh out of packaging; cars
zoom, bikes vroom, trucks boom on Y-roads ribboned round
primeval swamp revamped into prime real estate.
i know there's more
than high-rise concrete leggo, palms in a mail-ordered row,
adults busy as cartoons, teens lighter than balloons.
There's more, i know.
But from Ponce de Leon to the most recent pensioner
there's been one lure to Florida: eternal youth, eternal play.
Impossible. But past reason, child-deep. Wishes R Us.

Miami: more to it
than plastic-aluminum-chrome devices, playboys, six-digit toys,
push-button-flash experiences, winking drive-by existences.
There's more.
Below these bright surfaces
are primordial lives, a dinosaur's desires,
fears in the swish of water grass, movements you cannot click off,
night crawlings onto asphalt, a watchful, studded sleekness,
taut, ready to snap.
Miami.

See all this, if you want,
as the perennial clash:
people>|<nature, city>|<bush,
in agonistic, mutual encroachment.
Or, from a deeper want, look deeper.
The cars, roads, buildings
that press down, that overlie
the marshes and their denizens
are toys to gadget out the underlying sense
of futile purchase, futile chase
of perpetual adolescence.

While, from the mind's dread swamps,
feared things slash to the surface,
slither, crawl from the crepuscule subconscious.
To these, our ancient presences,
toys are us.

And toys we remain, unless,
from a priceless cherishing
of our ordained aging unto inevitable death,
we nurture the unperishing
within, the everglades of consciousness.

All this is so clear
from the high window perspective
of Mount Sinai's ICU, where,
swaddled in beneficent technology,
your loved one sleeps back to you
from a journey to the boundary
of bright road and dark water.

Strange — but perhaps not —
that in a hospital in Miami
you glimpse — beyond a physician's,
even a metaphysician's view —
how — because Love is how as well as why —
to live, not always longer but always
more.   Ever   more

CROOKED BASKET SONNET
(for Sonia Williams)

Sometimes you feel the quintessential yearn of poetry
more in a flawed, less finished poem like a crooked basket
than in the intricating weave and accumulating symmetry
of one perfectly crafted; its braided lines, form, function – set.
For what else can you do with that perfection but admire?
And admiration will always intimate a subtle distancing.
Whereas the glitch of an unrhythmed word will wince, require
you go closer to the woven interstices, squint at the warped spacing

between sound and sense. In that niggling space is meaning.
This worrying at words, trying to fold, nip, twist them into designs
induces a life-deep dissatisfaction with the imperfect, an intense yearning
for all strands of everything to fit – like well-made basketry where the mutual clasp
     of strands entwines
beauty and usefulness. More rare in poetry. But a flawed poem twinges, twists
     a returning
to our quintessence: to braid, in flawless basketry, our selves, these frayed, uneven lines . . .

GAME. SET. MATCH

(a poem for two voices)

Mervyn	Morris
poetry	topanorris
word swerving	so tell
you i	start spin
look out	look in
He'll hide	his s(kill)
his game	he'll glide
a slant rhyme	past you
play you	until
you doubt	your I.
Word-sleight	will give
him mastery	you love
and finally	you love
how each time	the poet
makes you see	(almost, not quite,
too late)	in the final set
how, always, he	is serving

poetry

READING WORLDS

(for all the festival staff – and the wonderful students)

When i get home, everyone will ask me: "How was Amsterdam?"
And i'll begin to speak, then pause. Like an unfinished poem.

i went there so you could hear and read my world in poetry.
But what would have made it all more full, more true,

is if i could have heard and read your world in your world's words.
Because i couldn't, i began to look and listen for the other codes

in which a people inner-scribe, each day, without fuss, their literature.
i heard, then felt, your name-sounds: Willemijn, Matthijs, Floortje …

so many others… A language with a softened clomp and lurch
yet a familiar flow. Its very name, a hardness softening: Dutch.

North Amsterdam street-sounds were subdued, the evening their best fit:
bike tyres whispering, a small boat on a canal muttering, "Piet, Piet…"

In Amsterdam, sights spoke to me, unworded, more than sound.
Images – quick sketches or slow, layered paintings – came into mind:

an unexpected spurt of bicycles, left corner of the eye, gushing
past me to a far intersection, then multicoloured splatterings diminishing;

a near-naked Barbie twitching a finger in a glass window in the district,
looking, behind eyes of mirrored glass, seeing who'll buy the act;

a quiet bend in a canal, a weathered houseboat, three ducks nodding past –
a mysterious nostalgia, almost restful, for something i had lost.

But it's my first time in Amsterdam. How can I feel reminiscence?
Then it comes to me. The image pricked the sweet-sharp ache, the wince

of that stinging, ineradicable desire for everything, somehow, to fit.
And poetry is the constant hurting promise and possibility of that.

Since the Read My World Festival, i've thought more about poetry translation,
how each poem, in each language, has a translucent shadow, a ghostly twin

in every other language; and how the words of conjuring translators
invoke them, flesh them again, bring them, new-found relatives, to meet us.

i'm thinking more now of what's gained, not lost, in translation
and of how poetry, mother of literature, can twin us, Holland//Caribbean.

i think of the Amsterdam ferry, its to-and-fro between shores, untiring;
of that blunt boat and its frothing wake as sail-makers' tools, repairing

one side to another, a movement following a rhythm and strict lines
always in pairs, for the companionship, and sometimes oblique rhymes,

translating people back and forth, a journey strenuous and necessary.
i'm thinking that poetry, for us, could be that ferry.

But i still wish i could have read your world in Dutch in Amsterdam.
And till i can translate this one, it's an unfinished poem.

DEAR

My mother, like others of her generation when buying an item,
might say, her purse out but still unopened, "This is too dear."
And the word falls now on the floor of memory, a soft pang, a dull gleam,
like a coin that dropped and rolled a little, wobbling toward a shut door.

                              'Dear'. The different tremorings in the word.
In primary school, learning to write a letter, you began straightforwardly, 'Dear –'
And not that long before the salutation trembles in ambivalence: 'Dear John – '
The word, unsaid, can quiver a clenched jaw: a general on the eve,
watching the departing soldiers and not saying: 'This will cost us dear.'
There is a question always whispered underneath its utterance: How much?
How much do you value … this? them? him? her? us? me? How much?
Further within the word, deeper than its sounding, a fore-echoing of a demand.
Did any of this hesitate my mother's hand held over the unopened purse?
No. The simple, strict arithmetic of domestic economics would have been enough.
Yet i can't help pondering: the entanglings of history leave knots in a language
and her era, unravelling, might entwine persons and shop items, rendering both 'dear'.
The coin rolls along memory, wavering to the door.
Stops. The door opens and – quietly, just after it – shuts.
What the image means – who dropped the coin, who opened the door, shut it,
what is the room – can be snarled easily in clever answers, convoluted chat.
But i know i and my generation don't say items are dear. They are expensive.
And i wonder what word, locked beyond light in our innermost recesses,
most truly names the value – how much – we feel of things, of others, our selves,
this…

SUNDAY

Sunday morning, quiet as pastures,
peaceful as cows standing so still
they look like boulders in the distance.
There've always been Sunday mornings like this,
when God became young again,
and looking back you see
that childhood was a Sunday morning.
Now you see it, only now,
in the Thursday of your life,
waiting for the week's end.

Next door, some last night's fool,
twitchy from the spasmic choreomania
that jumped up votaries of Saturn's Club get up to,
half-drunk, turns up his set full-blast,
scattering the blackbirds that were pecking nearer,
hanging over on my Sunday.

As for me, sometimes a poem, brighter-feathered,
will alight, tip-tap closer for a while, then fly
to someone waving far across a quiet pasture.
And I walk back across my field of days,
following as best i can below,
toward a Sunday and a child,
ever more familiar …

This Sunday, though, in ordinary time, is passing —
time to do some work.

TY NEWYDD
(for Sally and Elis)

What comes to mind now are the lines of drystone walls
along some of the roads or scribbled on fields around.
Whether they marked the ways there in strict rhyming couplets
or loped in free verse rise and fall around a croft,
they were solid, structured – and they had a cadence.
I could feel it, though i had never pondered why.
But you had told me once. You'd watched him build a wall –
Elis, your husband – and understood it was not only craft
but a tradition, blood-quick, bone-strong, flexing his fingers
to find the next stone, then the next, fitting into the rhythm
of a syntax he could feel but could not head to before hand.
All these lapidary lines, written in manual script on countryside,
follow a measure, yet are – in the truest sense – not planned.
They shape themselves exactly, without the clot of mortar, by true fit
of stone to stone, in the integrity of elegant, well constructed sentences.
Yet, pondering now the heft and strive of earth – aeons – to make the right
stone come into his hand, i wonder whether my life's ground can stand
the shock of inner geological rift, the difficult geography, harsh weathering
that have to happen for its broken surface to yield rocks for building.
In words older than Welsh, these walls spell me a hard and necessary teaching.
i envy Elis. Handling random fragments, with deep structured grace, into a usefulness
with beauty. That's art. As for poems, a poet has to be first a wordwright.
Then, perhaps, poetry. Lines of obdurate, enduring words upholding one another
through the best fit, the best sequence. An occasional chink of light.

THE BLUE OF ONE'S WEIRD

Friday night on Jeremie St, a pale blue deepening to midnight, as i hurry
for what could be the last bus, hunched in a sullen wait, kerbside,
among the peanut shells, scrunched wrappings, cigarette ends, a stray dog,

a man flicks the dead end of a dry sandwich – to an instantaneous flurry
of rats that quiver and squeal, that spurt in grey blotches, that swift-slide
back to the creviced dark behind car tyres, or scud down a slimed gutter.

i try to zigzag quickly through the night-people, but an infra-blue thin fog
is hazing everything; their movements drawl, smoke-slow, their voices mutter;
Jeremie St, unstiffening from the day, seeps past like something leaking.

A dreamflow, that was glared out in the day's dazzle, now swirls to clog
the usual crosscurrents frothing between our selves; the blue drift, with an
         othering flutter,
blurs the flat lines and slick day-glo colours of our week-squinted sight.

Slo-mo, the night ones lean away from, then sidle toward me, seeking
what their days lack, what our daily trafficking in the hot blaring light
drives from our public ways into the dark dwindling bush of our dreaming.

They're talking as they drift – but of what and to whom they're speaking
they seem not to know. And though what they're looking for is there with insight,
their eyes, blank dials, are registering nothing, staring through a glaze.

The housing blocks around are shut dark – except for one lit window,
         like a silent screaming.
That is the sound. The one that we loudly unlisten as we buzz through our
         bright daze.
It is the dreamdeep unheard howling for eternity that ghosts our every action,
         every word.

It is that sound, though they have never heard it, which draws the night ones, streaming
along emptying streets, talking and gesturing past each other through a blue haze.
Until they flow beyond me and the fog clears. But now my whole life seems blurred.

i reach the bus. All bleared. I wonder if even one of these late travellers has ever heard . . .
It's possible – but not likely, i think, as we move off. It's not everyone's weird.

KINDLING

O hard flint of my intellect,
O cold stone of my heart,
what can strike you together
hard enough, long enough
that, when i least expect,
a spark will quicken, start
a fire in these dried twigs of dead acts,
this chaff that words are now?
How long must I collect
this tinder-trash i am; accumulate,
lifelong it seems, the dry-split
brittle hoard of it?
And yet if i would choose, endure –
but how? And how hard! –
the clash of iron rock and flint,
then their gash, their grating
might in a flash, alight
on my small desperate heap of years,
and, kindling, transform them to an offering:
flame-licked, swallowed, consumed, all
in a longed for, feared, self-annihilating,
self-annealing fire.

WALKING

Though you seldom notice,
each footstep you take
crosses an abyss,
a possibility of falling
into nothing.
Think how easily
(a slip, there to here)
how unexpectedly
(a trip of thought
just now – then now)
one step to the next
a stumbling happens.
You fall, you flail against the falling, you fall
further than the ground no longer now beneath you.
Where you were going is gone. Out of your mind
falls memory, intention; all you know is a no,
a no-don't-fall, don't
drop so far down; you go
below all that you thought
you were but may not be
son/brother/sister/daughter/mother/father/employee of/employer of/ student/
out of work/fan of/friend of/lover of/owner of –
owner of …
you flail to not fall so far down you come to know you are
owner of nothing
and therefore nothing
therefore no thing
therefore all

TIDES

1

At the black sand estuary, the sea's tide ebbing and you with it.
The ineluctable withdrawal of the water and in you a draining.
No desire to do more than draw breath – and only enough
to allow for such life as sea moss might have, holding to rock.
If the sea now tides away from you, leaving the shoreline
shabby and paltry with the bits of what has finally been exposed
as you, so be it. So be the lies, half-lies, the twisted ends
of rusted wires of small malices; so be the warped plastic objects,
their cracks your half-smiles; so be the limp wrinklings of latex
pinched between stones without a flutter, your spent fantasies;
so be the ugly, pocked-silica, grit-barren bits of chipped, resenting self,
unloved and unlovely. So. See them all as the sea pulls itself back from you,
leaves you a detritus of near-despair. Yet – a gift, if you accept.

2

How? Do not demand the sea smooth these uglinesses, wish-washes them
into sand, bland them under a surface placidity, a calming seemliness
that does not last. That desire secretes a sly oil slick, thickening
toward the estuary in soft, slow death. Better to accept your debris. Look
at thin, flat disposable cutlery dropped and casual brittle promises;
at pettinesses of Styrofoam cups, cartons, your light acquaintances discarded;
at zags of half-buried broken bottles, their glints your unenacted cruelties.
Accept. As best – and when – you can. Look at your waste.
Soon the sea's unfolding onto black sand will again cover this refuse
because to see this, be this only, would despair you. So accept as well
the necessary mercy of the waves recovering you after the waters just unveiling.

3

Tides. Systole and diastole. The inhalation-exhalation always of existence
and the why of it least known when you most think you know,
most known when you least think it, when you feel most you do not understand.
Tides. The yes-no argument-agreement of sea-and-land. Suffer your self between,
endure that difficult place, a where that is a when that you cannot point to
more than a moment, the edge of wrack and waves returning   you.

RESOLUTION IN JANUARY

i look back on a year of uncompleted things. i see
hacked saplings, half-felled trees, pools of stagnant water.
i know how this happened. i know why. i know
that knowing's not enough. Somehow resolution
(which remains unknowable) … didn't happen.
Or not long enough. i'd begin to clear a way,
hack through interlocking branches
of gnarled thoughts, cutlass the strangling vines,
the soft asphyxiations of slow apathy,
then, in the undimming space, pause
too long.

        Always – i wish it were otherwise –
that pause. i wish there was no need. Always
afterward, the choices. And no choice to not choose.

        In that pause
of moment, a hum – the overhead wires quizzing
and a far question, heard, again

        In that pause
something as simple as sweetening/not sweetening tea
can hold your hand holding a spoon   over an abyss

        That pause,
infinitesimal, infinite, cannot remain unfilled. Fill it
your self, or fall into the interval

        i'm in now
looking at the half-completed path of the last year.
Avoiding making choices, they have made/unmade me.

                           Knowing this
is not enough; and knowing this is not enough
is not enough – then what, how, resolution?

                         In the inevitable interval
holding spoon, cutlass – feeling their weight, waiting, listening:
the powered humming above your head always   always

AFTER RAIN

A fitful rain, its tentative applauding
on zinc roofs moon-wet already in my neighbourhood,
and in such mornings, earlier than the sun's first light,
i am awake and yearning for awakening.

                    This happens
not every fo'day morning but at least
once, perhaps twice, a week: i wake
aching to be awoken. Sometimes, briefly, i am.

                    The rain's trickling applause
drops, becomes a patter, then a slow clap,
then almost the quiet of just after
the world's buzzed crackling has hushed
in you – but not quite; and not yet
the silence.

                    Someone still wants the rain,
the rush, the easy pleasuring of showers falling, it seems,
for you, wants even the secret bitter bliss
of applause drying down to a tap, an intermittent mocking
on the moon-leached roof. That, even that,
rather than silence.

                    Now the absence of the rain
is heavier than the rain. Now the wait, exact,
between expectation and imploring.

                    In that interval,
inevitable, the mind's dogs are milling –
its mongrels yapping, "How, how will it happen?"
its bred-for-attack dogs barking, "Who?"
Their harsh snapping, however, is how first you sense
the silence, how you know how near
the Stranger is. Listen

44

KEY

Each question, a key
put to the lock
of a black door – shut –
into the hoped for, feared.

No handle, latch. An aperture,
a puncture above a slit
– the small letter i –
admits to itself

one key, exact,
one question, twisting,
that clicks, cracks open
the black door, yielding

into a corridor, half-lit,
uncertaining your footsteps,
to around a corner, dim,
then black – a new door.

So always, the way in:
locked door, single eye,
crick of a key,
crack of an answer.

Till one day, one door,
one questioning key
transpiercing the small eye,
blinding uncertainty. See.

THE KING FISH

The question i am
is the hook that has caught me,
lifted me out of the sea;
is what i thrash and flail
to rid me of.
And yet the hook, the flesh,
the fighting to be free
are, together joined, all
necessary.
Straining to leap
beyond the hook's haul,
to reach past pain,
i leave what i thought
my element, and feel
the touch of light
directly. Only a glimpse,
only enough – just – to see
who asks the question
into me – of what i am –
is who I am
And then i fall
again, into the unlit sea.

HERONS

Where i live, herons are rare, the blue ones more so,
and i have never seen two herons, always one.
It is coming to me now that i do not expect to see them
the way i assume that blackbirds, finches, doves
come with the day. Instead, always when i am in the middle
of an ordinary action, a commonplace, about to cross a road,
or in the kitchen, just as i've closed the fridge and turned
around, maybe to go back to a half-empty plate, still warm –
there, within the kitchen doorway, frame of the familiar scene –
weathered bannisters below luffed mango leaves, my farmer neighbour's patch –
a shimmering, not so much appearing as seeming to have been always there.
A gleaming, wanting to withhold itself and almost doing that, almost
slipping back into the green, unnoticed but for the shift of light,
the shy, slight displacement of the tall grass by a greener, evanescent glimmering.

Another thought comes now: i have never heard a heron
call, squawk, warble, trill, make a slight, small sound
of any kind; so that i'm wondering, intrigued, half-seriously:
Do they? No? Yes, but not within the limitings of human presence?
And, half-fancifully, another thought: that it withholds its voice
because it knows its utterance would be lost in my translation,
and what it comes to say, if i could hear, would change my life.
It's whimsical, i know, a poet juggling images. Then
a blur of pale blue flashes underneath my eyelids,
a suddening of memory: olive-green river knuckled with rocks,
a track, crisp underfoot, only half-following the bank,
the drip of sunlight among branches, coppery tints in the low grass,
and at the river's edge, the rare blue unbelievability of it –
a blue heron in the moment before flight, tilted against time and its surrounding space,
standing in the flow of water, gripping soft, shifting earth, wings flexing air,
then a blue flare exploding silently, a brief blink of sky just over water,
and in the oblique space left – light.
Years before that glimpse brightened into a wordless utterance of realization.

Years... the self-abrading friction of striking sparks to light, burn, fuse
        feeling-intellect-sensation
into the briefest incandescence of rare triune being; a living of that moment, more than
        world's worth,
when a blue heron aligns for ascension, though still at home in water-air-earth.

AIR

What else but gratitude
for a flappering of blackbirds blown into sight below the verandah eaves
as though a hand above, loosening, has let fall what it was holding

How not be touched
under the skin, lighter than felt, by a far wind arriving weightlessly
where you are, the uninsistent intimacy of air, its soft inherence, moving

How to praise
in ultra-language below the palimpsest of cultures, worded histories,
what stirs in the ruffled slow green of a breadfruit tree's nudged leaves

If not for this –
how it is here, how it is always – how could i even try, even in vain,
to praise what hides from our limning, what eludes, though gently, praise

SAY LIGHT

Say it, say this word
186,000 times
until your final dark.
Hope it into you
deeper than skin.
Will it
into capillaries you cannot see
as you see the veined leaf
of a croton or a coleus.
Yearn a deep translucence.
Say light
into you, travel it
through leaf, branch, stem
and know
a rooting trust
of, somehow, light
as an underglow,
in ground of you.

WORDPLANTING

This poem will soon end
and its true usefulness begin.
After its last word, resolve
to place, with care,
a seed, a bulb, a branch
into a clay pot, old jug,
whatever holds handfuls of dirt
for onion, kale, aloe,
any small green fountaining
of nourishing or healing.
Pour water lightly, resolve
you will not listen to,
not read again, this
– or any other – poem
till your forefinger and thumb
flick from themselves
their last soft rubbings of soil
in a fine gratitude
back, as all must, into earth

 resolve

ABOUT THE AUTHOR

Born in St. Lucia in 1952, he studied and lived in Jamaica in the 1970s, where he explored his talents as a poet, playwright and director. As a poet, his writing ranges across the continuum of language from Standard English to the varieties of Caribbean English and he has also written poems in Kweyol, his nation language. He works in traditional forms like the sonnet and villanelle as well as in so-called free verse and in forms influenced by rap and reggae. He has published six books of poetry and his work has appeared in journals such as *The Greenfield Review*, *The Massachusetts Review* and in anthologies such as *Caribbean Poetry Now*, *Voiceprint*, *West Indian Poetry* and others. He has also edited *Confluence: Nine St. Lucian Poets*, *So Much Poetry in We People*, an anthology of performance poetry from the Eastern Caribbean, *This Poem-Worthy Place*, an anthology of poems from Bermuda, as well as student anthologies from creative writing students at the Sir Arthur Lewis Community College where he was a lecturer in literature and drama until 2007.

He has participated in poetry workshops by Derek Walcott and Mervyn Morris. He has himself designed and taught poetry workshops in places such as Ty Newydd in Wales and the UWI Caribbean Writers Summer Workshop in Barbados.

He has performed his work in the Caribbean, Europe and America at events such as the Miami International Book Fair, the Medellin Poetry Festival, Calabash Literary Festival, Vibrations Caraibes, the Havana Book Fair among others. In 2007, he won the Bridget Jones Travel Award to travel to England to present his one-man dramatized poetry production, *Kinky Blues*, at the annual conference of the Society for Caribbean Studies. He has twice won the Literature prize in the Minvielle & Chastanet Fine Arts Awards, for many years the premier arts award scheme in St. Lucia. He has been the recipient of a James Michener Fellowship to study poetry and an OAS scholarship to study theatre.

He has also established himself as an innovative playwright and director, authoring eight plays, and directing scores of others, including his own *The Drum-Maker* (1976), *The Song of One* (1995) and *Triptych* (2000), all of which have been published in drama anthologies. In 1984, he co-founded the Lighthouse Theatre Company in St. Lucia, and has long been involved in all aspects of the dramatic arts on the island. He has toured with theatre productions in the Caribbean and the UK. At different times he has been involved as actor, director and administrator in Saint Lucia's contingents travelling to CARIFESTA.

In 2000, Kendel was awarded the St. Lucia Medal of Merit (Gold) for Contribution to the Arts. His present focus is to use his skills as a writer and dramatist to raise public awareness and contribute to active solutions of critical social issues.

ALSO BY KENDEL HIPPOLYTE

Birthright
ISBN: 9780948833939; pp. 124; pub. 1997; £8.99

The *Heinemann Book of Caribbean Poetry* described Kendel Hippolyte as 'perhaps the outstanding Caribbean poet of his generation'. Until the publication of *Birthright* his poetry had only been available in anthologies and slim collections which have been little seen outside St. Lucia. *Birthright* reveals him as a poet who combines acute intelligence and passion, a barbed wit and lyrical tenderness.

He writes with satirical anger from the perspective of an island marginalised by the international money markets in a prophetic voice whose ancestry is Blake, Whitman and Lawrence, married to the contemporary influences of reggae, rastafarian word-play and a dread cosmology. He writes, too, with an acute control of formal structures, of sound, rhythm and rhyme - there are sonnets and even a villanelle – but like 'Bunny Wailer flailing Apollyon with a single song', his poetry has 'a deepdown spiritual chanting rising upfull-I'. Whilst acknowledging a debt of influence and admiration to his fellow St Lucian, Derek Walcott, Kendel Hippolyte's poetry has a direct force which is in the best sense a corrective to Walcott's tendency to romanticise the St Lucian landscape and people.

Kwame Dawes writes: 'It is clear that Hippolyte's social consciousness is subordinated to his fascination with words, with the poetics of language, and so in the end we are left with a sense of having taken a journey with a poet who loves the musicality of his words. His more overtly craft conscious neo-formalist pieces are deft, efficient and never strained. Villanelles, sonnets and interesting rhyming verse show his discipline and the quiet concentration of a poet who does not write for the rat race of the publishing world, but for himself. One gets the sense of a writer working in a laboratory patiently, waiting for the right image to come, and then placing it there only when it comes. This calm, this devotion is enviable for frenetic writers like myself who act as if there is a death wish on our heads or a promise of early passing. Our poetry, one suspects, suffers. Hippolyte shows no such anxiety and the result is verse of remarkable grace and beauty.'

Night Vision
ISBN: 9781845232351; pp. 80; pub. 2005, 2014; £8.99

Kendel Hippolyte speaks through and beyond tradition. He writes in sonnets and villanelles, in idiomatic dramatic monologues that capture the rhythms of Caribbean speech, in blues and rap poems, in free verse that draws upon the long-breath incantatory lines of Ginsberg and contracts in miniaturist forms as concise as graffiti.

In the title poem of this collection Kendel Hippolyte lays down an ambitious challenge to himself and his reader:

"Because we see with history,
it is difficult to see through it. And yet we must
or we become it, become nothing else but history."

In rising to meet his challenge, Hippolyte draws upon all his verbal mastery and critical insight to draw sharp focus upon a nation in flux, where urbanisation expands and fragments his home of St. Lucia. The poet turns his vision upon the people, the land and the culture, and finds a microcosm of the Caribbean in the 21st Century.

Fault Lines
ISBN: 9781845231941; pp. 78; pub. 2012; £9.99

If you want to feel what it's like to live on a small island, vulnerable to the wounded thrashings of world capitalism in crisis, an island where livelihoods are destroyed at the flourish of a Brussel's bureaucrat's pen, where Paradise is a tourist cruise ship come to remind you of your neo-colonial status, where global consumerism has poisoned the ambitions of the young into drugs, crime and violence, then the poems in *Fault Lines*, dread, urgent prophecies of "a black sky beyond", are indispensible guides.

With the verbal urgency of Ginsberg's "Howl", a visionary imagination that shares the company of Blake, *Fault Lines* confirms Kendel Hippolyte's reputation as one of the Caribbean's most important poets. What he does brilliantly is catch in the same poem both a precision of observation and the indeterminacy of the observing mind, the awareness that "whatever drove us was also banishing/what we were driven to". And there is not only that kind of doubleness, but the stunning ability to create poems that appear to observe themselves in their moment of creation, like "Silverfish" with its radical truth that "the secret all empires must suppress, in order, to metastasize into empires" is "the I-magination [that] lives beyond our ordering and is our ordering."

Awarded the 2013 OCM Bocas Prize for Poetry